Foundations of Our Nation

ESTABLISHING THE AMERICAN COLONIES

by Tyler Omoth

FOCUS READERS

WWW.FOCUSREADERS.COM

Focus Readers is distributed by North Star Editions:
sales@northstareditions.com | 888-417-0195

Produced for Focus Readers by Red Line Editorial.

Content Consultant: Dr. Gideon Mailer, Associate Professor of History, University of Minnesota Duluth

Photographs ©: akg-images/Newscom, cover, 1; North Wind Picture Archives, 4–5, 7, 8, 10–11, 12, 15, 16–17, 19, 23, 25, 27, 29; Red Line Editorial, 21

ISBN
978-1-63517-245-4 (hardcover)
978-1-63517-310-9 (paperback)
978-1-63517-440-3 (ebook pdf)
978-1-63517-375-8 (hosted ebook)

Library of Congress Control Number: 2017935900

Printed in the United States of America
Mankato, MN
June, 2017

ABOUT THE AUTHOR

Tyler Omoth grew up in the small town of Spring Grove, Minnesota. He has written more than 40 books for young readers. Tyler loves watching sports, particularly baseball, and getting outside for fun in the sunshine. He lives in sunny Brandon, Florida, with his wife, Mary, and their feisty cat, Josie.

TABLE OF CONTENTS

CHAPTER 1

PLANTING ROOTS

In 1584, Sir Walter Raleigh received important news from England's queen. She had given him permission to **colonize** North America. This would allow English people to sail across the Atlantic Ocean and start new lives. But North America was not empty. It was already home to many American Indian nations.

Sir Walter Raleigh did not travel to North America, but he made two voyages to South America.

The British did not believe they needed American Indians' permission to create colonies there.

Raleigh himself never went to North America. But he paid for others to go. They started the colony of Roanoke in 1585. It was on an island off the shore of present-day North Carolina.

The settlers had difficult lives. They were not able to grow enough food. As a result, the colony lasted only a few years. Some of the settlers returned to England. Others decided to stay. However, they were never heard from again. England's first colony in America had ended in failure.

In 1587, colonists celebrated the birth of the first English child born in North America.

In 1607, the English tried again. This time, approximately 100 settlers traveled to what is now Virginia. This area was home to the Powhatans, an American Indian tribe. The English settlers started a small colony on the Powhatans' land. They called it Jamestown. Sometimes the colonists traded with the Powhatans for food and other supplies.

John Smith meets with members of the Powhatan nation in the early 1600s.

Other times the two groups fought. Many colonists died from disease or hunger.

In 1608, John Smith became the leader of Jamestown. He asked the Powhatans for food. However, the Powhatans were worried about losing more of their land. They captured Smith but eventually set him free. After Smith attacked their villages, the Powhatans gave the colonists food. The colonists would have starved without it.

In the 1610s, the settlers began growing tobacco in Jamestown. This plant was in high demand all around the world. Soon, tobacco was a key part of Jamestown's **economy**.

The Powhatans taught the colonists how to grow crops. These lessons helped the settlers survive the difficult winters. Jamestown became the first successful English colony in America. The colonists raised crops and traded with England. This success led the English to send more settlers to America.

CHAPTER 2

THE *MAYFLOWER* ARRIVES

In September 1620, a ship known as the *Mayflower* set sail from Plymouth, England. The people on this ship were looking for a new start. They disagreed with the ideas of the Church of England. But they were not allowed to practice their beliefs in their homeland. They planned to start new lives in America.

People aboard the *Mayflower* say a prayer before leaving for America.

The settlers planned to sail to Virginia. However, the *Mayflower* arrived many miles north of its destination. The ship landed at Cape Cod in what is now Massachusetts. The settlers had been at sea for two months. They had dealt with storms and crowded conditions. So, they decided to stay where they were. They

THE *MAYFLOWER*

PASSENGERS
50 men
19 women (3 pregnant)
14 young adults (ages 13–18)
19 children (ages 12 and younger)
1 baby born on the voyage

SUPPLIES
water
sugar
rice
oatmeal
meat
cheese

named their colony Plymouth after the city they had left in England.

The settlers created a set of rules for their new colony. These rules became known as the Mayflower Compact. Each man had to sign this agreement before he could get off the ship. Women did not have equal rights, so they did not sign the agreement.

William Bradford became the leader of the colony. But life was not easy for the settlers. They had arrived in November. That meant they had no time to grow crops. The colonists lived aboard the *Mayflower* through their first winter. Many did not survive.

The Wampanoag tribe lived nearby. One of the tribe's members made contact with the settlers. He helped the settlers build peaceful relationships with the Wampanoags. Over time, the Wampanoags taught the settlers how to grow crops. They also showed the settlers how to gather food and hunt wild animals.

At the end of the summer, the settlers harvested their first crops. They celebrated with a three-day feast. This celebration became known as Thanksgiving.

The colonists would not have survived without help
from American Indians.

CHAPTER 3

EXPANDING THE COLONIES

By the mid-1600s, both Jamestown and Plymouth were successful colonies. England began to **claim** more land along North America's east coast. And more people left England to live in the new colonies.

France, Spain, and the Netherlands also claimed land in North America.

Dutch colonists gather in the city of New Amsterdam, later known as New York.

None of these countries asked for permission from the American Indians who had lived there for centuries.

In the 1670s, England took over the Netherlands' territory. The English renamed the area New York. In the 1680s, William Penn started the colony of Pennsylvania. Penn was part of a religious group known as Quakers. He left England because he wanted religious freedom. Penn encouraged other settlers to come to his colony. They made use of the area's farmlands and woods. Many people grew grains such as wheat and corn. They also raised animals. The colony grew quickly and became successful.

William Penn started the city of Philadelphia along the Delaware River in 1682.

Other colonies developed farther south. People in these colonies grew cash crops. These are crops that farmers sell for a profit.

The colonies of Virginia and Carolina were known for their tobacco farms. However, this crop required huge amounts of **labor**. Farm owners brought in thousands of enslaved Africans in the late 1600s. The farm owners forced them to work on farms without pay. This allowed the farm owners to make more money. Slavery existed in the northern colonies, too. But it was most common on southern farms.

By the early 1700s, England had numerous colonies in North America. Each colony had its own government. Each colony also used its own money. The colonies often traded goods with one another. Over time, England's American colonies grew and prospered.

ECONOMIES OF THE COLONIES

PENNSYLVANIA
wheat and corn

NEW HAMPSHIRE
wood

NEW YORK
fur

MASSACHUSETTS
ships

RHODE ISLAND
whale oil

CONNECTICUT
flour and fish

NEW JERSEY
cattle

DELAWARE
fish

MARYLAND
fish

VIRGINIA
tobacco

CAROLINA
tobacco and rice

AMERICAN INDIANS AND COLONISTS

As colonists arrived from England, they often met American Indians who were already living in the area. American Indians sometimes gave English settlers the right to live on pieces of land. But they did not want the settlers to own it.

The colonists encouraged American Indians to speak English and follow English **customs**. In many cases, colonists pushed American Indians off their own land. They even attacked Native villages for food.

In 1633, a member of the Wicomesse tribe sent a letter to the governor of Maryland. The letter said colonists should not force American Indians to change their ways. Instead, the colonists should change their ways. "You are here strangers and come into our country," the letter said.

Colonists often tried to force their language, religion, and beliefs on American Indians.

"You should rather **confine** yourselves to the customs of our country, than **impose** yours upon us."

CHAPTER 4

UNITING THE COLONIES

England united with Scotland in 1707, and the new country became known as Great Britain. Leaders in Great Britain found it harder and harder to maintain control over the colonies. Each colony operated differently from its neighbor. This made it difficult for Great Britain to **enforce** its own laws.

British troops patrol a colonial city.

Great Britain also had problems with other European countries. For example, France claimed a territory known as the Ohio Country. But Great Britain also claimed this area. To settle the matter, the two nations went to war. The conflict became known as the French and Indian War (1754–1763). Both sides got help from different American Indian nations. In the end, Great Britain won the war. The victory gave the British large amounts of new territory.

The war had a major effect on the British colonies. They were no longer threatened on every side by other European countries. This greatly

British soldiers march through Pennsylvania during the French and Indian War.

improved the colonies' security. However, the security came at a cost. The war had been very expensive. British leaders expected the colonies to help pay for it.

As a result, Great Britain created new **taxes** on everyday goods. For instance, the Sugar Act raised taxes on products such as sugar and molasses.

The Stamp Act raised taxes on printed documents. The Tea Act raised taxes on tea.

Many colonists did not think Great Britain had the right to tax them. In 1773, a group of colonists fought back. They boarded three British ships in Boston, Massachusetts. The ships were stocked with valuable tea. The colonists threw it overboard. This event became known as the Boston Tea Party. It was a protest against the tax on tea.

Great Britain responded with a series of new laws. They took away power from the colonies. Many colonists strongly disagreed with the new laws.

Colonists destroy tea to protest a tax that British leaders created.

In 1775, these disagreements led to war. A year later, the colonies made an announcement. They no longer wanted to be ruled by Great Britain. They wanted **independence**.

FOCUS ON
ESTABLISHING THE AMERICAN COLONIES

Write your answers on a separate piece of paper.

1. Write a paragraph that describes the main ideas of Chapter 4.

2. Do you think the Powhatans should have helped the Jamestown settlers? Why or why not?

3. Who became the leader of the Plymouth colony?

    A. William Bradford
    B. Sir Walter Raleigh
    C. William Penn

4. How did the French and Indian War help the British colonies?

    A. It helped many colonists earn more money.
    B. It led to a series of new taxes on the colonies.
    C. It removed the threat of other European countries.

Answer key on page 32.

GLOSSARY

claim
To say something belongs to someone.

colonize
To settle in a new place and take control.

confine
To limit or stay within.

customs
Ways of living.

economy
A system for buying and selling goods.

enforce
To make sure something happens.

impose
To force others to accept something.

independence
The ability to make decisions without being controlled by another government.

labor
Work that a person does.

taxes
Money added to the cost of a purchase and given to the government.

TO LEARN MORE

BOOKS

Heckt, Jackie. *Immigration to Colonial America.* New York: PowerKids Press, 2016.

Lusted, Marcia Amidon. *The Jamestown Colony Disaster: A Cause-And-Effect Investigation.* Minneapolis: Lerner Publications, 2017.

McAneney, Caitie. *Uncovering the Jamestown Colony.* New York: Gareth Stevens Publishing, 2017.

NOTE TO EDUCATORS

Visit **www.focusreaders.com** to find lesson plans, activities, links, and other resources related to this title.

INDEX

Answer Key: **1.** Answers will vary; **2.** Answers will vary; **3.** A; **4.** C